science fair

Science Alive!
Light

CRABTREE
Publishing Company
www.crabtreebooks.com

How to use this book

Each chapter begins with experiments, followed by the explanation of the scientific concepts used in the experiments. Each experiment is graded according to its difficulty level. A level 4 or 5 means adult assistance is advised. Difficult words are in boldface and explained in the glossary on page 32.

Crabtree Publishing
www.crabtreebooks.com

PMB 16A, 350 Fifth Avenue,
Suite 3308, New York
New York 10118

612 Welland Avenue,
St. Catharines, Ontario,
Canada L2M 5V6

**Published in 2002
by Crabtree Publishing Company**

Published with Times Editions
Copyright © 2002 by Times Media Private Limited

Series originated and designed by
TIMES EDITIONS
An imprint of Times Media Private Limited
A member of the Times Publishing Group

Coordinating Editor: Ellen Rodger
Project Editors: P. A. Finlay, Carrie Gleason
Production Coordinator: Rosie Gowsell
Series Writers: Darlene Lauw, Lim Cheng Puay
Series Editors: Oh Hwee Yen, Lek Hui Hui
Series Designers: Loo Chuan Ming, Geoslyn Lim
Series Picture Researcher: Susan Jane Manuel
Series Illustrator: Roy Chan Yoon Loy

Cataloging-in-Publication Data
Lauw, Darlene.
    Light / Darlene Lauw & Lim Cheng Puay.
      p. cm. — (Science alive)
    Includes index.
    Summary: Presents activities that demonstrate how light works in our everyday lives. History boxes feature the scientists who made significant discoveries in the field of light.
    ISBN 0-7787-0560-9 (RLB) — ISBN 0-7787-0606-0 (pbk.)
    1. Light—Experiments—Juvenile literature. 2. Optics—Experiments—Juvenile literature. [1. Light—Experiments. 2. Optics—Experiments. 3. Experiments.]
I. Lim, Cheng Puay. II. Title.
QC360 .L385 2002
535'.078—dc21
                                                                   2001042423
                                                                        LC

Picture Credits
Marc Crabtree: cover; Bes Stock: 7 (bottom),10, 27 (bottom), 30 (bottom); Cordon Art B.V., Holland: 31 (top); Easycam Workshop: 22; Getty Images/Hulton Archive: 7 (top), 11 (top), 15, 23 (top), 23 (middle), 27; Photobank Photolibrary Singapore: 1, 14 (bottom); Pietro Scozzari: 23 (bottom); Science Photo Library: 11 (bottom), 14 (top), 18, 19, 26 (top), 26 (bottom), 30 (top), 31 (bottom); Travel Ink: 6

Printed and bound in Malaysia
1 2 3 4 5 6—0S—07 06 05 04 03 02

INTRODUCTION

What is the fastest thing on Earth? How do we see things around us? These questions relate to light. Light is the most important form of energy on Earth. Light is both a **particle** and a wave. Find out more about light by doing the science experiments in this book. You will learn how to bend light, make your own camera, and even form a rainbow!

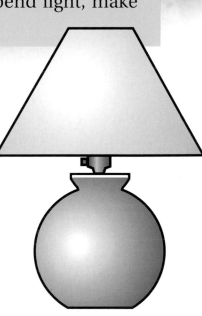

Contents

Why is my reflection moving away?

A reflection of light occurs every time light hits a surface. Light reflects differently on smooth and rough surfaces. The color and material of a surface influence the reflection of light off the surface. Have you ever noticed that your mirror reflection moves away from you as you move away from the mirror? Find out why!

You will need:
- A small poster
- A bathroom mirror
- Tape
- A measuring tape
- A manual focus camera

Mirror, mirror on the wall

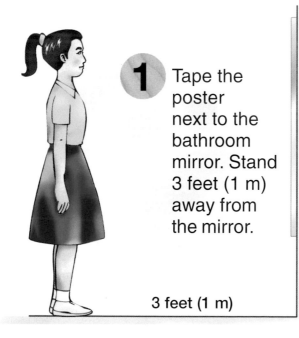

1 Tape the poster next to the bathroom mirror. Stand 3 feet (1 m) away from the mirror.

3 feet (1 m)

2 Focus the camera on your image in the mirror. (Ask an adult to help you focus the camera if you are not sure how to do it yourself.)

3 Next, point the camera at the poster.

4 Without changing the focus of your camera, move backward until you see the image of the poster clearly in the camera. Mark your position with tape.

5 Using the measuring tape, measure the distance between your marked position and the wall. It should be exactly 6 feet (2 m), twice your original distance from the mirror. Since you were standing 3 feet (1 m) from the mirror, this means your reflection was also 3 feet (1 m) from the mirror! Try other distances and see if you get the same results!

6 feet (2 m)

What is light reflection?

Light reflection occurs when light waves, called rays, hit and bounce off a surface. Groups of light rays are called beams. The angle at which light beams hit a smooth surface, such as a mirror or glass, is called the **angle of incidence**. The angle that light beams bounce off, or reflect off, the surface is called the **angle of reflection**. The angles of incidence and reflection are the same, or equal. This is known as regular reflection, or the first law of reflection.

The mirror experiment showed regular reflection. In the experiment, the distance of three feet (one meter) between you and mirror was the same as the distance between your reflection and the mirror. So your reflection was six feet (two meters) away from you. The camera was focused on your reflection six feet (two meters) away. That was why when you looked at the poster from only three feet (one meter) away, it appeared out of focus. But when you were six feet (two meters) away, the poster looked clear.

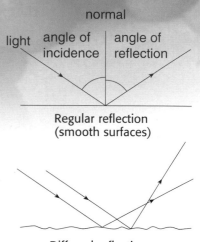

normal

light — angle of incidence | angle of reflection

Regular reflection
(smooth surfaces)

Diffused reflection
(rough surfaces)

Glass windows reflect the sky and the buildings across the street.

Euclid and the laws of reflection

Euclid was a Greek mathematician who lived in Alexandria, Greece at around 300 B.C. Euclid discovered the laws of light reflection and wrote his findings in a book called *Optica*. Euclid also wrote a series of mathematical books known as *Elements*.

This was his most important contribution to the scientific world. *Elements* has thirteen volumes. It covers many aspects of mathematics such as geometry and the properties of numbers. Even today, many high schools use a modified version of Euclid's *Elements*.

◯UIZTIME

Can Uncle Bob use a mirror to help him find out how tall he is?

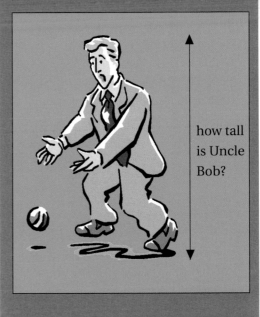

how tall is Uncle Bob?

Answer: Yes, if Uncle Bob can see the full length of his body, from his head to his feet, in the mirror's reflection. The height of Uncle Bob's reflection in the mirror will be half his height. So if Uncle Bob's reflection is three feet (one meter) tall, his real height will be six feet (two meters).

Did you know?

Side view mirrors on cars (*below*) curve outward to give drivers a wide view of the traffic behind them.

🌍 SPYING MIRRORS

Some mirrors allow us to see through them from one side. These mirrors are made from reflective glass. Many stores use one-way mirrors to monitor their customers and to spot shoplifters. Shoppers are often not aware that they are being watched. Store owners should inform shoppers so that they do not invade other people's privacy. One-way mirrors should not be used to spy on people.

I can bend light!

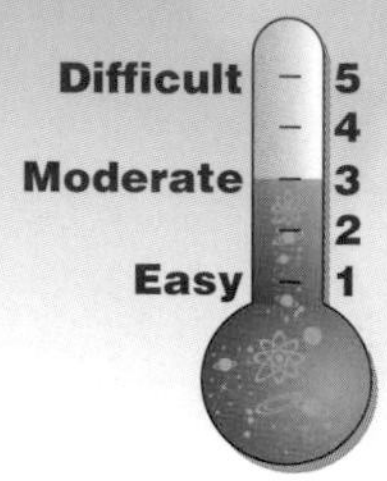

Y ou can control the path of light.
All you need is a small mirror,
and, of course, light!

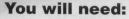

You will need:
- A small piece
  of cardboard
- Scissors
- Tape
- A flashlight
- A pencil
- A sheet of paper
- A mirror
- A piece of
  plasticine
- A friend
- A protractor

I can control light!

1 Cut a small slit in the
cardboard with the scissors.
Tape the cardboard to
the flashlight.

2 Using the pencil, draw a line
across the middle of the sheet
of paper. Place the mirror at
this center line and stick it in
position with plasticine.

3 Turn off the lights in the room.
(Pull the curtains if the room is not
dark enough.) Shine the flashlight at
the point where the center line touches
the mirror. Ask your friend to hold the
flashlight. Then use the pencil to trace
the path of the flashlight and the
reflected beam.

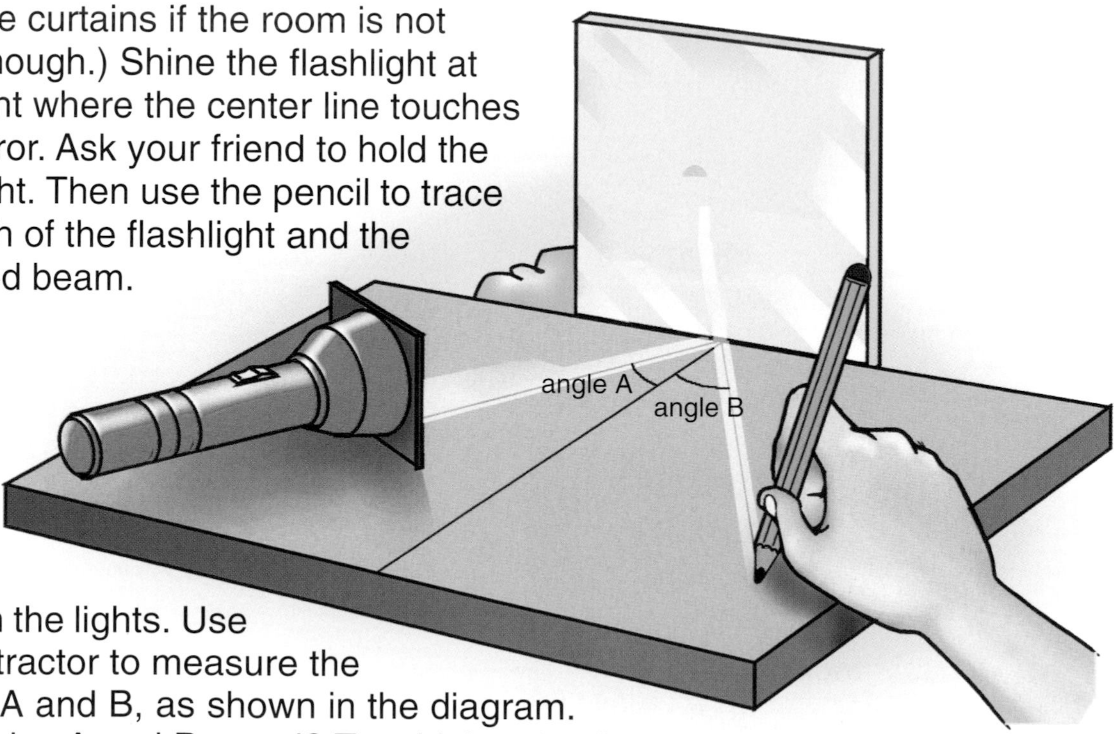

angle A

angle B

4 Turn on the lights. Use
the protractor to measure the
angles A and B, as shown in the diagram.
Are angles A and B equal? Try shining the flashlight at
different angles and see if the same thing happens!

8

Now that you know how to control the path of light, why not try to bend light! Try this magic trick.

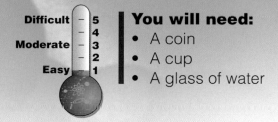

Difficult — 5
— 4
Moderate — 3
— 2
Easy 1

You will need:
- A coin
- A cup
- A glass of water

The mystery of the reappearing coin

1 Place the coin at the bottom of the cup.

2 Look at the coin. Keeping your head still, move the cup away from you until you no longer see the coin.

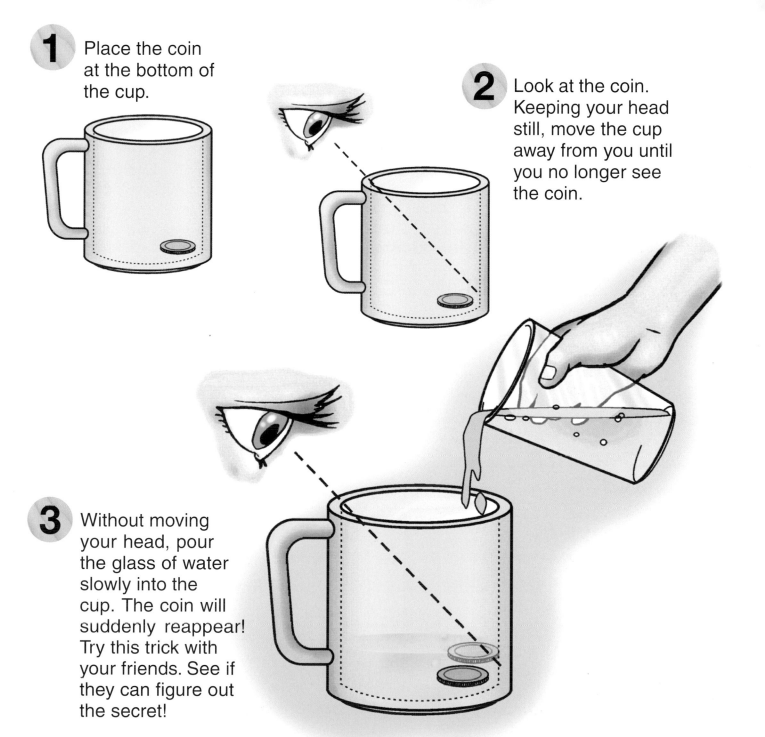

3 Without moving your head, pour the glass of water slowly into the cup. The coin will suddenly reappear! Try this trick with your friends. See if they can figure out the secret!

9

What is light refraction?

Light rays bend when they pass from one material to another. This bending is called **refraction**. Refraction happens because light travels at different speeds in different materials. Light changes its speed when it passes from one material into another. It travels at lower speeds through dense materials such as water and at higher speeds through materials that are less dense. As the speed of light decreases, the angle of refraction decreases as well. (*See diagram above, right.*) In the experiment *The Mystery of the Reappearing Coin*, the coin appeared closer to the surface than it really was. This was because light that reflected off the coin bent, or refracted, as it left the water. In this case, the refraction created an illusion or a **mirage**.

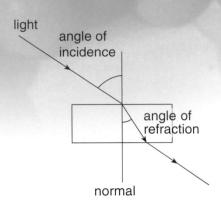

light
angle of incidence
angle of refraction
normal

The tiles in a swimming pool look curved because of refraction.

Who discovered refraction?

In 1621, Dutch mathematician Willebrord van Roijen Snell (1580–1626) discovered the law of light refraction. He based his findings on an earlier theory of light by French mathematician René Descartes (1596–1650; *left*) and his own experiments. The equation for calculating refraction is known as Descartes' Law in France, and Snell's Law elsewhere.

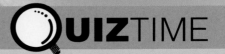QUIZTIME

Predict how this light ray will emerge from a container with sides made of mirrors. Check the answer on page 15!

Did you know?

Optic fibers (*below, left*) are very thin strands of glass that can transmit light. The **diameter** of each fiber ranges from 0.0005 to 0.005 inches (about 0.013 to 0.13 mm). Compare this to human hair, which is about 0.002 inches (0.05 mm) thick! By inserting optic fibers into the body, doctors can see what's inside without performing surgery. Engineers also use optic fibers to examine parts of machines which cannot be seen with the eyes. Today, optic fibers are even used to transmit telephone calls!

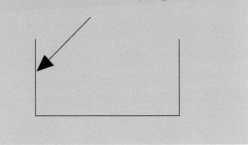

PEPPER'S GHOST

Magicians, movie directors, and some other entertainers rely on light to create illusions. In 1862, Professor Henry Pepper was the first to create a stage illusion, now called Pepper's Ghost. Pepper used light and an angled piece of mirrored glass to produce the illusion of a ghost floating on a stage. Pepper's Ghost appeared on stage in London during a play, and was one of the first special effects used in theater. It became a popular technique for plays and later for movies.

Wonder of light

Have you ever wondered how rainbows are formed? Where do they come from? The best time to see a rainbow is after a heavy rain. Do you know why? The experiments here will tell you the answers.

Make your own rainbow!

Difficult — 5
— 4
Moderate — 3
— 2
Easy — 1

You will need:
- A large, shallow bowl
- A small mirror
- A pocketknife
- A sheet of cardboard
- A sheet of white paper

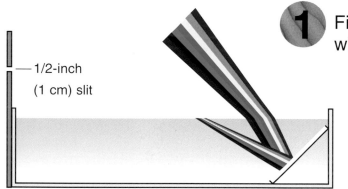

1/2-inch
(1 cm) slit

1 Fill half of the bowl with water.

2 Place the mirror in the water so that it rests in one corner on the side of the bowl. The reflective side of the mirror must face upward.

3 Ask an adult to help you cut a slit 1/2 inch (1 cm) wide in the cardboard. Position the cardboard near a window. Place the bowl beside the cardboard. Make sure that sunlight passes through the slit and lands on the mirror.

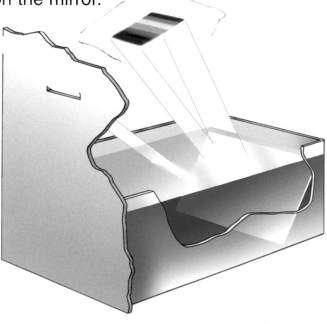

light from the window passes through the slit

4 Hold the sheet of white paper above the bowl. Aim the reflected beam of light from the mirror onto the paper by adjusting the angle of the mirror. Do you see a **spectrum** of colors? Congratulations! You have just created a rainbow!

You can be an artist who paints with light. Learn how to create a spectacular light painting. This experiment works best in a dark room.

You will need:
- A sheet of white paper
- A flashlight
- A glass bottle

Paint with light!

1 Place the bottle between the piece of paper and the flashlight as shown in the diagram.

2 Shine the flashlight through the bottle.

3 Move the flashlight back and forth until you can see a rainbow on the sheet of paper.

4 *Voila!* You have made a multicolored light painting!

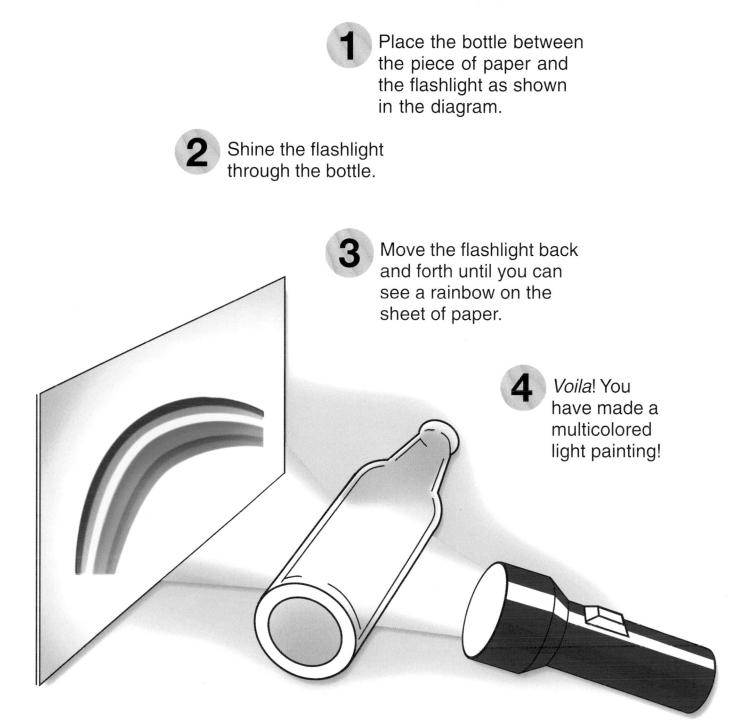

Splitting light

The light we normally see is called white light. Its name is misleading because it appears white, but is really a mixture of colors called a spectrum. A spectrum is a multicolored band of light containing the colors red, orange, yellow, green, blue, indigo, and violet. These are the same colors we see in a rainbow.

When white light passes through a **prism**, it splits into seven colors.

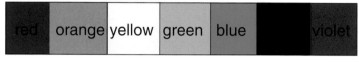

| red | orange | yellow | green | blue | | violet |

Spectrum of white light

Humans can only see white light. Some animals can see beyond the spectrum. These animals see a longer spectrum with **ultraviolet** light at one end after violet light, and **infrared** light at the other end. Bees, for example, can see ultraviolet light. Rattlesnakes can see infrared light. Humans do not see infrared light, but they feel it as heat.

Raindrops are spherical, or rounded, and symmetrical, or balanced. Light passing through a raindrop splits into a circle of seven colors. If the ground was transparent, we would see a circular rainbow, not just a semi-circle!

Sir Isaac Newton

In 1666, Sir Isaac Newton, a British mathematician and scientist, used a rectangular block of glass known as a prism to split light. Newton placed the prism near a slit in his window shutter. When light from the slit passed through the prism, it fanned out into a band of different colors. Newton placed another prism beside the first in the path of the band of colors. This combined the spectrum into white light again! Newton also discovered the laws of motion and is thought to be one of the world's greatest scientists.

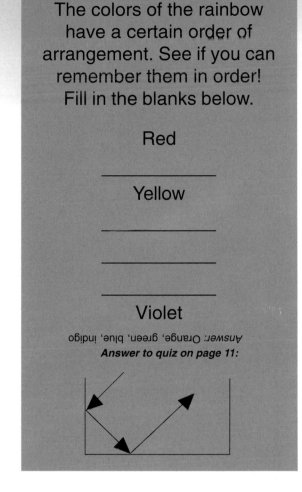

QUIZTIME

The colors of the rainbow have a certain order of arrangement. See if you can remember them in order! Fill in the blanks below.

Red

_____

Yellow

_____

_____

_____

Violet

Answer: Orange, green, blue, indigo

Answer to quiz on page 11:

Did you know?

Rainbows happen when sunlight shines through water droplets. The droplets reflect and refract the light rays, making the colors disperse into a spectrum. Rainbows always move with the observer. Try looking for a rainbow the next time it rains.

OILY RAINBOWS?

After a rainy day, oil from vehicles forms small oil slicks in puddles of water. You can see "rainbows" in these oil slicks. These colorful bands appear because of the refraction of light. When light enters the oil slicks, the slicks act like prisms and split the light into its different colors. Small oil slicks on the road are not as harmful to the environment as huge oil spills in the oceans. These oil spills usually happen when oil tankers leak. The oil pollutes the water in the oceans and poisons the food that fish and other marine animals eat. It can take decades for an ocean habitat to recover from an oil spill.

Nothing escapes my eyes!

Submarines use light reflection to see above the water's surface. People in a submarine can see what is above the water by looking into a **periscope**. What is a periscope? Try this experiment to find out how a periscope works.

Difficult — 5
— 4
Moderate — 3
— 2
Easy — 1

■ **Ask an adult for help**

You will need:
- A pocketknife
- A cardboard tube 20 inches (50 cm) long
- Two small mirrors
- Glue or tape
- A 45-degree triangle

Be a submarine captain!

1 Use the pocketknife to make a horizontal slit about 4 inches (10 cm) from each end of the cardboard tube. Ask an adult to help you. The length of the slit should be three quarters of the tube.

2 Using the 45-degree triangle, measure 45 degrees from the horizontal slit. Cut two slopes as shown in the diagram.

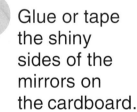

3 Glue or tape the shiny sides of the mirrors on the cardboard.

4 Your periscope is now ready! Use it to look over walls. Can you see what is happening on the other side of the wall?

By positioning the two mirrors the right way, you can see things normally hidden from your view. There are many other fun tricks you can try with two mirrors. Here is another activity!

The never-ending series

Difficult — 5
— 4
Moderate — 3
2
Easy — 1

You will need:
- Two small mirrors
- An eraser

1 Place the eraser between two mirrors.

2 Hold both mirrors upright. Look into one mirror to see the image of the eraser on the opposite mirror. Adjust the angle of your sight until you see many images of the eraser in the mirror. Now, try it with other objects!

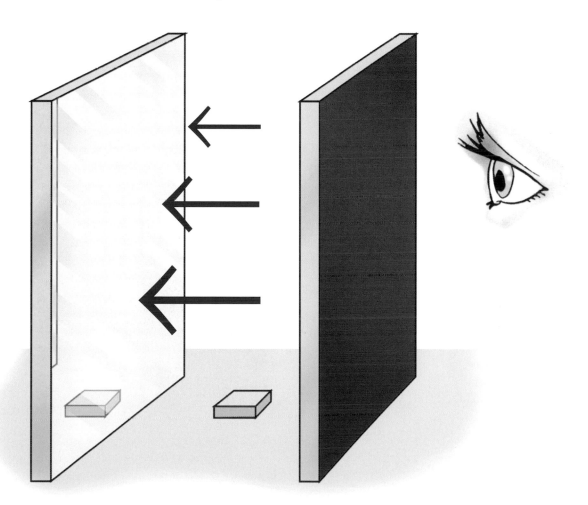

How periscopes work

Periscopes let you see things that are far away or hidden around corners. They work on the principle that light is reflected at the same angle it hits a surface. A mirror placed at 45 degrees to the path of light will reflect the light beam at an angle of 90 degrees.

Periscopes are used in submarines so that the crew can see what is above the water. A submarine's periscope may have a tube 50 feet (15 m) long and only ten inches (25 cm) wide. If there are only two mirrors on either end, the final image will be too small to see. Images can be made bigger by installing **lenses** in the tube. The lenses enlarge the final image the crew sees through the periscope.

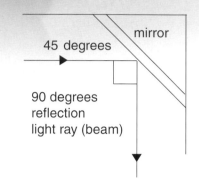

Repeated reflections

In the second experiment, *The Never-ending Series*, the reflection of the eraser bounced off the two mirrors repeatedly. This is why you saw many reflections of the same eraser in the mirror!

The first submarine

In 1620, the Dutch inventor Cornelis Drebbel built the world's first submarine. It was a small vessel built with an outer hull of greased leather over a wooden frame. The submarine carried twelve oarsmen and several passengers below the Thames River in England for several hours. A series of tubes supplied air from the surface for the people to breathe.

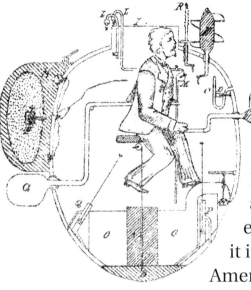

The first military submarine was an egg-shaped craft called the *Turtle* (*left*). David Bushell, an American engineer, invented it in 1775 during the American Revolution. The *Turtle* had no air supply and had to rise to the surface every 30 minutes. This made it difficult for the *Turtle* to carry out its intended task: to lay a mine below a British ship during the Revolution.

Did you know?

Periscopes are used to see nuclear reactors in nuclear power stations (*left*). Nuclear reactors produce dangerous chemical emissions and **radioactive** waste. Viewing them through periscopes reduces the risk of chemical and radioactive poisoning. The world's longest periscope is at the National Reactor Testing Station in Idaho. It is 90 feet (27 m) long.

QUIZTIME

Peter wants to see what Andy is doing at the back of the room without getting near him. Can you help Peter position four mirrors so that he can see Andy? Check the answer on page 23!

Peter

Andy

NIGHT VISION

Night vision devices have special lenses that capture and translate infrared light into a form humans can see. The military uses these devices in submarine periscopes to allow them to see in the dark. Policemen use night vision to track down crime suspects and check crime scenes for clues that humans cannot see using their eyes alone.

How does a camera take pictures?

A camera takes pictures by reflecting light! You can make your own camera with these simple instructions.

Difficult – 5
 – 4
Moderate – 3
 – 2
Easy – 1

You will need:
- A pencil
- A paper or plastic cup
- A piece of tracing paper
- A pair of scissors
- Tape
- A piece of cardboard

Make your own camera!

1 Using the pencil, make a hole in the center of the bottom of the paper cup. Trace the open end of the cup on the piece of paper.

2 Draw tabs around the outline, then cut it out. Fold and tape the tabs around the open end of the cup.

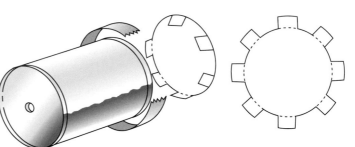

3 Cut and wrap the piece of cardboard around the paper used to trace the cup. Tape it firmly.

4 Aim the camera at a bright object, for example, a table lamp. Do you see an **inverted** image of the object on the tracing paper? You have made a pinhole camera!

20

There is another way to copy real life objects exactly the way you see them!

Difficult – 5
– 4
Moderate – 3
– 2
Easy – 1

You will need:
- A picture
- A large piece of glass
- A table lamp
- A sheet of drawing paper
- A pencil
- A friend

Instant art!

 Position the picture, drawing paper, glass, and the table lamp as shown in the diagram.

 Shine the lamp on the picture. Hold the glass upright with one hand. Look through the glass from the side of the picture. Shift your head until you see an image of the picture on the drawing paper.

3 Trace the outline of the picture with the pencil. You can adjust the size of the picture by tilting the top of the glass toward the right or left. Ask your friend to hold the glass if you need both hands to draw. Compare your drawing with the original. Are they similar?

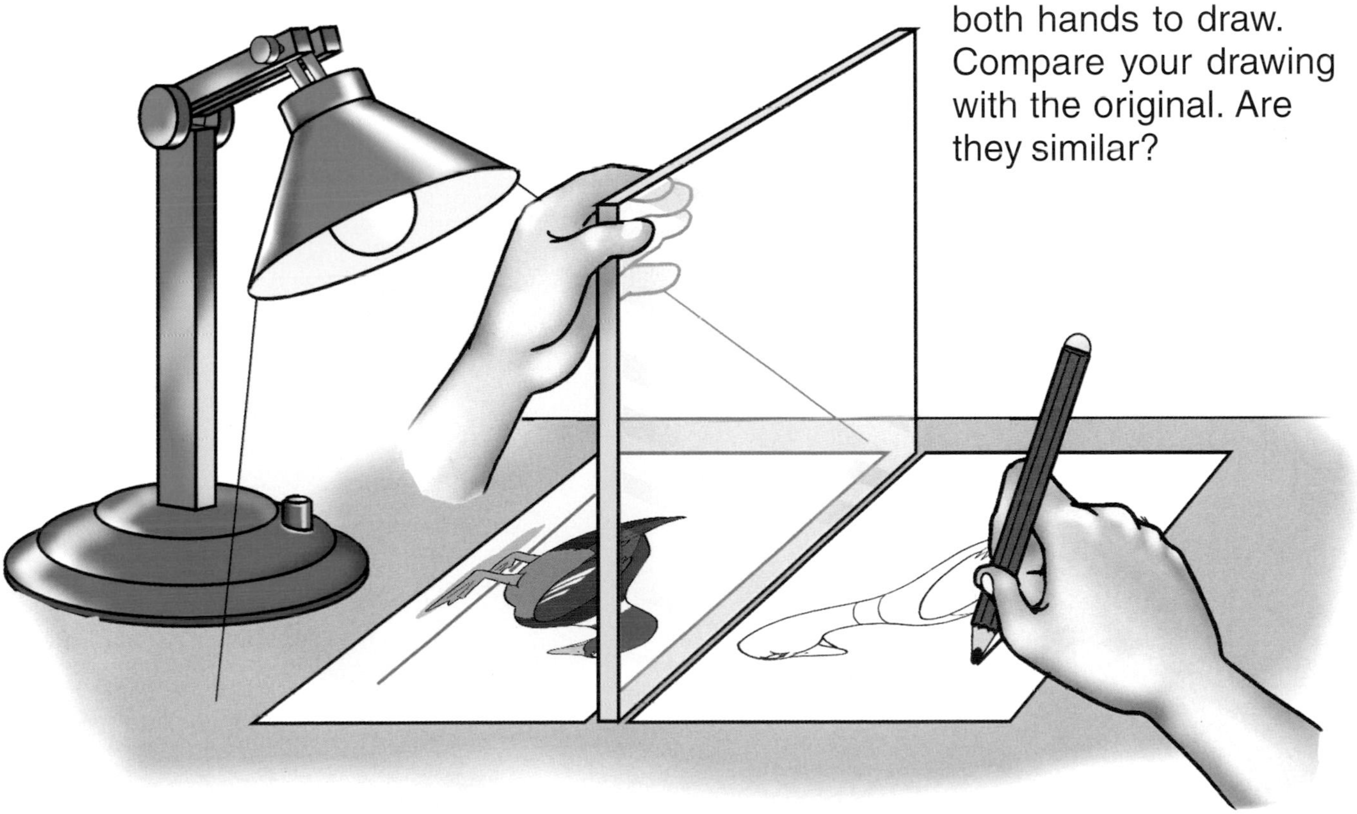

How a pinhole camera works

Light travels in a straight line. In the experiment *Make Your Own Camera*, light from the bottom of the lamp passed through the small opening. It emerged from the opening and appeared at the top of the screen. Similarly, rays from the top of the lamp appeared at the bottom of the screen. The final image on the screen was therefore upside down and reversed from left to right.

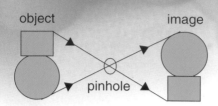

How a pinhole camera works

Instant art

The diagram on the right shows how light reflected from the picture to your eyes in the experiment *Instant Art*. The bright light from the lamp caused the glass to be reflective, like a mirror. Unlike a mirror, you could still look through the glass to trace the outline of the image onto the paper.

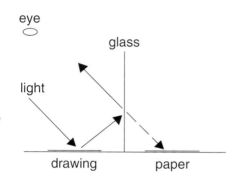

A photographer takes a picture with a single-lens reflex (SLR) camera. SLR cameras allow the user to focus manually. Do you use manual or automatic cameras to take pictures?

Camera Obscura

Since the 1500s, scientists and artists have known that light passing through a small hole in a dark room will form an inverted image on an opposite wall. This dark room was known as the Camera Obscura. Placing a lens at the small hole made the image sharper. By the 1700s, artists began using a portable box with a lens in place of the room to record images for their drawings.

Early cameras were huge and bulky. Some measured up to 16.5 feet (5 m) wide! Modern cameras are very small. The camera on the right is the world's first spy camera. It was made in 1960.

Try to draw the image of the candlestick when it passes through the pinhole camera. See page 31 for an example.

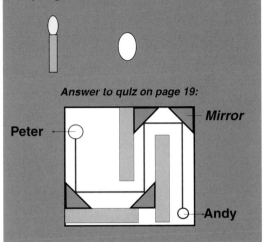

Answer to quiz on page 19:

Peter — Mirror — Andy

Did you know?

Modern cameras (*above*) work on the same principle as the Camera Obscura. They record images coming through glass or plastic lenses onto light sensitive film. The film is then developed into a picture when we add certain chemicals to it. Using special film, we can now develop images taken from pinhole cameras.

SPY CAMERAS

With modern technology, spy cameras can be as small as belt buckles. Private detectives use these cameras to take pictures without being detected. Many shopping malls use small surveillance cameras as part of their security systems. These cameras are hidden from the shoppers' view. Tiny spy cameras make it easy to spy on people, but invading other people's privacy is not always the right thing to do.

The colorful kaleidoscope

Kaleidoscopes are fascinating instruments that use reflection to form beautiful patterns. Did you know they never form the same pattern twice? Artists and designers sometimes use kaleidoscopes to get ideas for new patterns!

A pattern that never repeats itself!

1 Ask an adult to help you buy the two mirrors from a glass or hardware store. Ask the store salesperson to smooth and tape the edges of the glass so that the glass is safer to handle.

Difficult 5
4
Moderate 3
2
Easy 1

■ **Ask an adult for help**

TAKE CARE!

The sharp edges of the mirrors can cut you. Do not try to cut them yourself. Ask an adult to cover the sharp edges with several layers of tape before you handle them.

You will need:

- Two mirrors of the same size: 8 X 2 inches / 20 X 5 cm
- Scissors
- A cardboard sheet
- Tape
- Tracing paper
- Glue
- Transparent plastic film of various colors
- A protractor

2 Using the pair of scissors, cut a piece of cardboard the same size as the mirrors. Tape the mirrors and the cardboard together as shown in the diagram. The shiny surfaces of the mirrors should face inward.

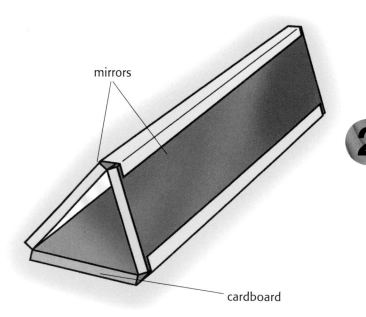

mirrors

cardboard

3 Cut a piece of the tracing paper to fit over one end of the kaleidoscope. Glue it in place.

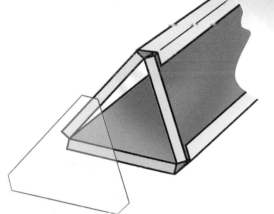

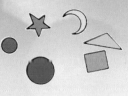

4 Cut the transparent plastic film into as many shapes as you can think of. Use as many colors as you can.

5 Place the colored pieces of film in the tube. Hold the tube upright so that the pieces are resting on the tracing paper.

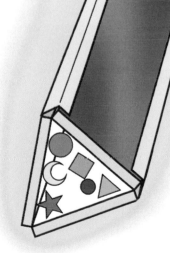

 6 Look down into the kaleidoscope. Do you see a pattern? If your kaleidoscope is made properly, the pattern will have six identical sections. Jiggle the kaleidoscope to form new patterns!

How a kaleidoscope works

The patterns (*right*) formed in kaleidoscopes are the reflections of the mirrors inside the tube. Mirrors arranged differently give very different images. The number of sections in a kaleidoscope depends on the angle between the mirrors.

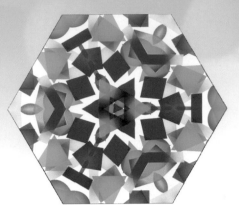

A glass maker at work. Liquid glass is very hot. The glass maker has to wear a helmet and very thick gloves to protect himself against the heat and sparks.

History of the kaleidoscope

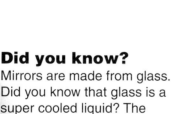

Sir David Brewster (1781–1868), a Scottish scientist, invented the kaleidoscope in 1816. The name "kaleidoscope" came from the Greek words *kalos*, meaning beautiful, *eidos*, meaning form, and *scopos*, meaning wonder.

In the early 1870s, Charles Bush, an American, improved Brewster's design and made the kaleidoscope popular.

Did you know?

Mirrors are made from glass. Did you know that glass is a super cooled liquid? The mixture of silica and lime forms a very thick liquid that behaves like a solid. If you take a close look at some of the huge glass windows in very old buildings, you will find that the glass is slightly thicker at the base of each window! This is because the glass had gradually flowed downward after hundreds of years!

QUIZTIME

Can you guess the number of sections for each kaleidoscope below?

	Angle between mirrors	Number of sections
A	10	
B	20	
C	30	
D	60	
E	90	

Answer: 36 (360/10 degrees), 18 (360/20 degrees), 12 (360/60 degrees), 6 (360/60 degrees), 4 (360/90 degrees)

PROTECTIVE GLASS

The windshields of cars are made of special glass. During a collision, a car's windshield (*above*) will shatter into many tiny pieces but will not fall apart. The broken glass remains in the frame of the windshield. This prevents the glass from cutting the driver. Some banks have bulletproof glass walls to protect bank staff from armed robbers. The bulletproof glass is also made of the same special glass of car windshields.

I cannot believe my eyes!

An illusion is something that is different than it appears. What our eyes see is sometimes very different from what is actually there. Try this activity to see an example of an illusion.

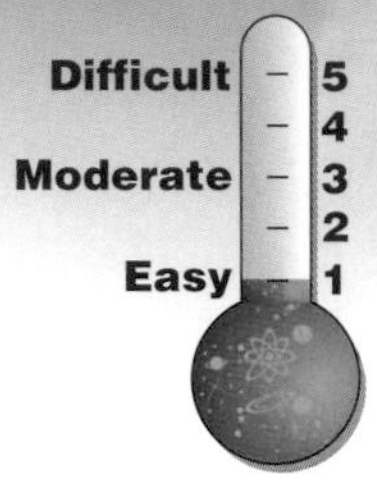

Is seeing truly believing?

1 Take a good look at the two curved shapes below. Which is bigger? Ask your friends to see if they agree with you.

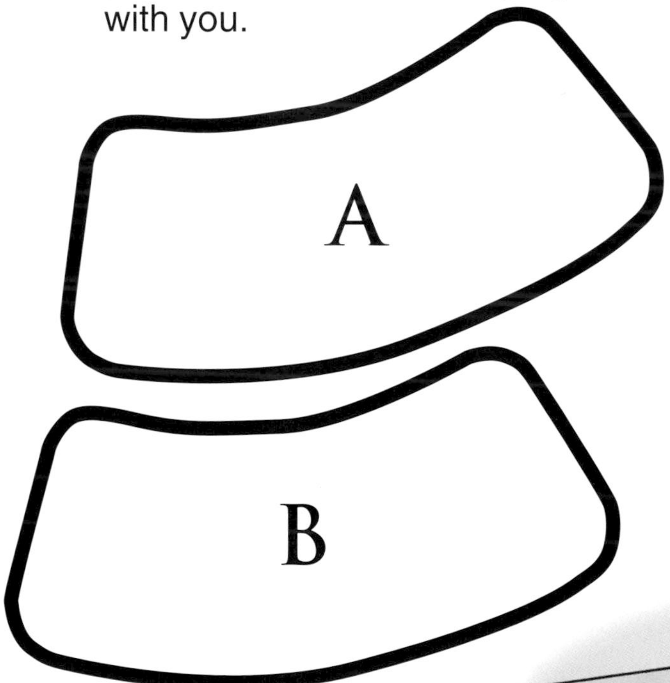

A

B

You will need:
- A ruler
- A piece of string

2 Measure how far the top and lower curves stretch for both figures. Use the ruler to help you, as shown in the diagram below. Can you see that the top curves of A and B are longer than their lower curves? Measure the size of the two figures. To do this, use the string to outline each figure. Then, measure how long the string is with the ruler. You will find that both figures are of the same size!

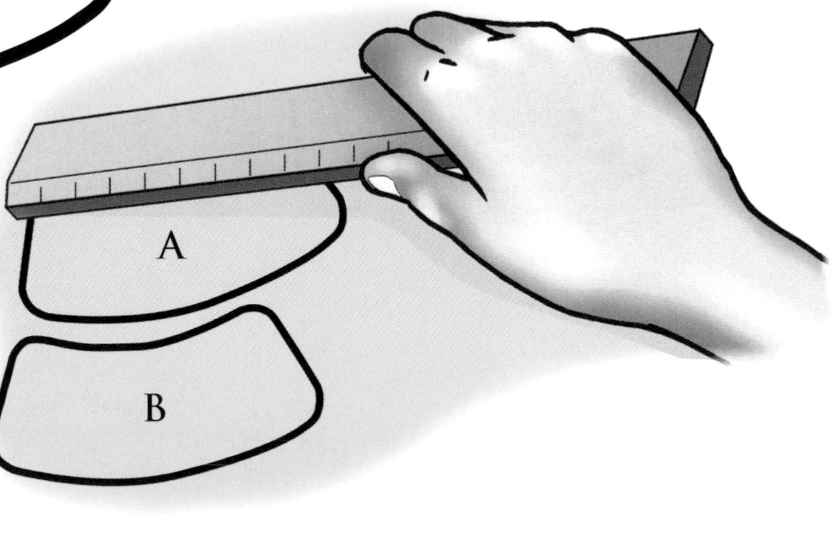

A

B

Imaginary letters!

Look at the illustration below. Can you see the word "optical?" Examine the figure very closely. The word is actually made up of black shapes, not letters! What is happening?

You will need:
- A piece of paper
- A piece of tracing paper
- A pencil

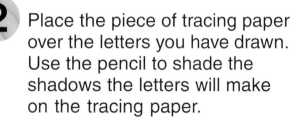

 1 On the piece of paper, draw the outlines of the letters o, p, t, i, c, a, l. Shade the letters with the pencil.

2 Place the piece of tracing paper over the letters you have drawn. Use the pencil to shade the shadows the letters will make on the tracing paper.

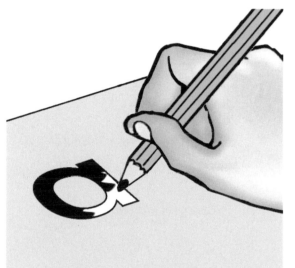

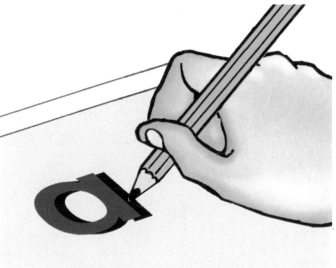

3 Remove the piece of white paper and look at your drawings on the tracing paper. Do you see the word "optical?" Try this again with other words!

optical

Optical illusions

Many **optical illusions** give the wrong impression about the size of one object compared to another. This happens because of the shapes of the objects and the way they are positioned. In the experiment *Is Seeing Truly Believing*, Figure A looked bigger than Figure B but the two figures were of the same size! Your eyes were tricked because Figure A's longer curve appeared just above the shorter curve of Figure B.

Look at the image above. Doesn't it look like it's moving?

Imaginary letters

Our brain always tries to interpret the information we receive from our eyes by comparing what we see now with memories of things we have seen before. In the experiment *Imaginary Letters*, our brain concluded that we were looking at the shadows cast by the letters in the word "optical."

What a large head! This picture is taken from above the boy. His head is closest to the camera, so it looks very big. Compare this to his feet. Do they look tiny? That is because they are farthest away from the camera!

An amazing artist!

Look at the picture on the right by M.C. Escher. This picture is called *Relativity*. Escher, a Dutch artist, was famous for his paintings of impossible

buildings. In his paintings, Escher placed objects such as staircases at odd angles. Escher had no formal training in mathematics or science, but his paintings show an understanding of mathematical ideas.

QUIZTIME

Read the phrase below. Is there a mistake?

Pansies
in the
the spring

Answer: The word "the" appears twice.

Answer to quiz on page 23:

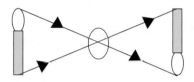

Did you know?

A laser (*left*) is a narrow beam of light made of one color only. Lasers have many uses, such as cutting through metals and in surgery. Scientists use lasers to measure distances such as the distance from the Earth to the moon. Cashiers in shopping malls and supermarkets also use lasers to read the bar codes on packages.

CAMERA TRICKS

Taking a photograph of an object from different camera angles can create different visual effects. Some companies make advertisements with low angle photography to make their product appear larger than its actual size. Trick photography is just one way to make a product appear more appealing to the customer.

Glossary

angle of incidence (page 6): The angle at which light hits a surface.

angle of reflection (page 6): The angle at which light is reflected off a surface.

density (page 10): The mass of a substance in a given volume.

diameter (page 11): A straight line passing from one side of an object, through its center, to its other side.

infrared (page 14): The part of the invisible light spectrum that is beyond red.

inverted (page 20): Something that is inverted is upside down.

kaleidoscope (page 24): An instrument that uses light reflection to create patterns.

lenses (page 18): Curved pieces of glass or plastic that distort the sizes or shapes of images seen through the glass or plastic.

mirage (page 10): An optical illusion, often caused by light refraction.

optical illusions (page 30): Images that appear different than what they are.

particle (page 3): A small part of matter.

periscope (page 16): A device that allows the crew of a submarine to view what is above the surface of the water.

prism (page 14): A piece of glass in the shape of a pyramid that can split white light into seven colors.

radioactive (page 19): Refers to substances that disintegrate and give off harmful waves or particles of high energy.

reflection (page 4): An image that is formed when light bounces off a surface.

refraction (page 10): The change in the path of light when it passes from one material into another. When a ray of light refracts, it bends.

spectrum of light (page 12): A range showing the individual components of light, both visible and invisible.

submarine (page 16): A vessel that can travel above and under water.

ultraviolet (page 14): The part of the invisible light spectrum that is beyond violet.

Index